IMAGES
of England

EAST STAFFORDSHIRE
NEEDWOOD FOREST
TO THE WEAVER HILLS

When old photographs show topographical scenes one can pay a visit and observe changes. With dated events, press reports usually supply interesting details. The only comment possible here, however, is that the photograph comes from the Mayfield area at the northern extremity of East Staffordshire and that, one hundred years later, such a charming study deserves to be recorded.

IMAGES
of England

EAST STAFFORDSHIRE
NEEDWOOD FOREST
TO THE WEAVER HILLS

Compiled by
Geoffrey Sowerby and Richard Farman

TEMPUS

Tempus Publishing Limited
The Mill, Brimscombe Port,
Stroud, Gloucestershire, GL5 2QG

ISBN 0 7524 0197 1

Typesetting and origination by
Tempus Publishing Limited
Printed in Great Britain by
Midway Colour Print, Wiltshire

A fine study of Romany families encamped by the Dove near Uttoxeter, *c.* 1904. These German gypsies (called *Zigeuner* – wanderers – in Germany) aroused sufficient local interest for Alfred McCann to record them for a picture postcard. Their camp site, with covered carts, traditional caravans and tents is enclosed by a portable screen. Our word 'gipsy' evolved from 'Egyptian', their supposed country of origin when first appearing in England in the sixteenth century.

Contents

Map showing the parishes within the Borough of East Staffordshire. As explained in the Introduction, this collection excludes Burton upon Trent and the urban area immediately adjoining. (Map courtesy of East Staffordshire Tourism.)

Introduction

In previous collections we have presented old photographic records of that portion of the Borough of East Staffordshire within and immediately around Burton upon Trent, a region now well covered by pictures and text.

This volume aims to complete a portrayal of the past in the rather neglected remainder of East Staffordshire – the delightful countryside of Needwood Forest, moving northwards through Uttoxeter to the Weaver Hills.

Scenes from Uttoxeter's past have indeed appeared in other publications but much of the rest of this extensive, mainly rural region has not received the attention it deserves. We have therefore concentrated, as far as possible, on views and aspects of Uttoxeter and its surrounding villages not previously recorded.

Just as with our Burton upon Trent selection, when we briefly crossed the river into Derbyshire in order to offer a more complete picture of the district and its characteristics, so with this volume we have occasionally crossed the Dove – the county boundary – to include a few Derbyshire scenes of places having close connection with East Staffordshire. The vagaries of the Dove are such that, for example, Tutbury station is in Derbyshire while Sudbury station was in Staffordshire.

Many places featured also have close and long-standing ties with Uttoxeter, the natural centre and market for much of the agricultural region, and having formerly been within the Uttoxeter Urban and Uttoxeter Rural Districts of the period 1898–1974. Much of the Needwood Forest area west of Burton was that of the former Tutbury Rural District. Local government reorganisation then established the present Borough of East Staffordshire (retained without further alteration in the latest review) based at Burton upon Trent.

Uttoxeter Town Council deserves commendation for continuing to promote interest in their portion of the Borough, establishing a Heritage Centre for the preservation of all aspects of the local scene and its history while Tutbury, too, has its own local museum, both well worth visiting.

Our hope is that this book will add a further contribution to the vital recording of times past. For some readers our East Staffordshire journey may be largely nostalgic; but we also trust that it will be found interesting and informative by those already familiar with this very scenic region of East Staffordshire while, perhaps, encouraging those less well acquainted with its attractions – as well as the growing number of visitors – to explore and discover it for themselves.

Needwood Forest once comprised well over 9,000 acres of woodland and common extending from Yoxall northwards to the Dove; and westwards from near Burton to meet Bagot's Park with its extensive woodlands. It was divided into four wards: Tutbury, Barton, Yoxall and Marchington. In each there was a lodge: Byrkley in Tutbury ward; Sherholt in Barton ward; Yoxall Lodge (rebuilt in 1951 as a farmhouse) and Ealand Lodge in Marchington ward. There were also ten parks separated from the forest area and named as follows: Castle Park, Rolleston, Stockley, Castle Hay, Barton, Sherholt, Highlands, Agardsley, Hanbury and Rowley. Needwood Forest was enclosed and largely disafforested in 1801.

One

Needwood Forest
and Bagot's Park

The Abbots Bromley Horn Dancers appear here in new costumes made locally in 1904 after a subscription list was organised by the vicar, Rev S. Berkley. Left to right: Harry Bentley; Jack Bentley (Fowell); Arthur Bentley (Fowell), 2nd Blue Horn; Albert Bentley (Fowell); George Blower, 2nd White Horn; David Bentley (Fowell); William Bentley (Fowell), 1st Big Blue Horn; Tom Sammons; Stanley Blower, 1st White Horn; Arthur Bentley, 3rd Blue Horn; William Martin; William Adey, 3rd White Horn. (Fowell family also known as Bentley). The largest of the horns weighs $25\frac{1}{4}$ lbs and is 39 inches across. A 'squeeze-box' provides the musical accompaniment.

Inns today need car parks and village streets have to be widened to cope with ever increasing traffic so that, since 1903, this part of Yoxall's Main Street as viewed from the Crown Inn and looking towards the church has undergone considerable alteration. The Crown is advertising itself as a 'Cyclists House'.

Though the layout of School Green remains there has been extensive new building beyond the large farmhouse (Leafield) on the right, while the property facing (left centre) has been restored and its timber framework revealed. Before Yoxall's present school was built in 1896 an old schoolhouse near here gave the location its name.

Except for country houses, interior scenes are scarce. This fine picture of an Edwardian farmhouse dining room remained unidentified for thirty years. From a set by Simnett of Burton, Leafield (on the right in the previous view) was identified when visiting Yoxall while researching for this book. It is likely that the photographs were taken when it was the home of the Roberts family. The room has been structurally altered but, as seen here, is full of splendid period detail as regards furniture, ornaments and pictures, one of which shows the Meynell Hunt meeting at Byrkley Lodge.

This splendid Edwardian caravan – 'Cosy Lodge' – belonged to Cecil Barrie, whose Empire Palace touring company were in the area around September 1909. Unfortunately even theatre museums seem to be short of information about these performers but the postcard, sent from Rugeley, records a visit to Yoxall, commenting: ' … this is the car of the people who were in that show at the School, Monday and Tuesday.'

The Meynell Hunt outside The Foresters Arms at Woodlane, Yoxall. In 1908 the landlord was only granted a renewed licence on acknowledging his 'statutory obligation to supply tea as well as liquor'. The little greens dividing the crossways have long since gone. In the centre background is the roof of the R.C. Chapel of St Francis of Sales, which recently celebrated the bi-centenary of its foundation in 1794/5.

The four ancient bailiwicks of Needwood Forest (Yoxall, Barton, Tutbury, Marchington) met at Hoar Cross. This is the cross roads outside The Meynell Ingram Arms, a People's Refreshment House (*c*. 1906). This association (est. 1900) promoted inns also serving refreshments and non-alcoholic drinks as opposed to the anti-public house lobby of some temperance organisations. The view shows the noted rose garden and lawn used for summer teas and games, now the car park.

The Old Hall, Hoar Cross, was noted in hunting circles for the Hoar Cross and, later, the Meynell Hunt. Subsequently the Church of England Children's Society established a 'Home of the Good Shepherd' (St Michael's), adapting the premises at the end of the last century. It remained a children's home until the early 1980s. This Simnett photograph shows a recreational scene in the grounds, *c*. 1904.

Richard Keene's photograph of the magnificent Church of the Holy Angels, Hoar Cross, erected 1872–1876 (architect G.F. Bodley) by the Hon. Mrs Meynell-Ingram in memory of her husband, Hugo Francis of Hoar Cross and Temple Newsam, Yorkshire. This is 1900, before the addition of pews; the floor being re-laid in black and white marble; a stone pulpit recessed into the pillar; and the screen raised to enhance the effect of height.

The home of the Meynell-Ingrams until 1951, Hoar Cross Hall (built 1862–71) has passed through several phases before becoming today's Health Spa Resort. This photograph by Simnett of Burton records the long gallery as it appeared in the early 1900s.

This is *c.* 1902 portraying the Needwood Forest countryside around Hoar Cross at that time and the nature of some of the quiet lanes that saw only foot and horse traffic and had been probably little altered within living memory. Ealand Brook and Mare Brook meandered along to form the River Swarbourn running down to Yoxall. Bridges and road improvements were soon to come with the new century.

Byrkley Estate sale catalogue (1913) described Needwood School, Newchurch, as 'a healthy site with spacious playground, school room 26 x 35 ft, partitioned class room, coat lobby, three wash basins and five detached privvies, conveniently divided.' The teacher's house had sitting room, kitchen, scullery, three bedrooms, good garden and water supply. It is now a private residence; the school, long closed and minus one bell tower, looks forlorn.

Christ Church in Needwood was built (in brick) to serve new settlers after the clearance of the Forest. It experienced a phenomenon in 1891 when a rare example of globe lightning passed right through the church. Demolished Byrkley Lodge features in a window while outside is the curious tombstone of John Tharme (died 1888): 'And a bugler he was of the very first order; Twelve years in New Brunswick's American Order … '.

Moving southwards to the parish of Wychnor, there is evidence of very early habitation in this area but it remains remote with its big house, Wychnor Park. The hall contains a wooden relic of a rare tenure dating back to John of Gaunt granting the manor to the Somervilles in 1340 on condition that a flitch of bacon be always retained in the house (except in Lent).

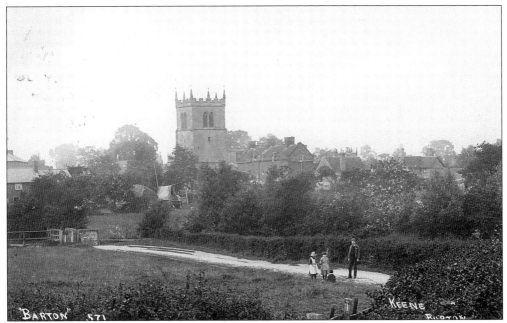

Barton from an unusual viewpoint by Richard Keene (*c*. 1902). In 1692 Barton was described as 'a good country town and hath several gentlemen and freeholders in it. The most remarkable thing is a fine chapel built by John Taylor this being the place of his nativity' – a cottage near the church site. Dr Taylor was chaplain to Henry VIII and the secondary school is named after him.

This photograph looks east from Barton church tower, *c*. 1914, probably on a Saturday afternoon as cricket is in progress. There is little new building, open countryside spreading across to Walton Hall just discernible on the hill. Below (left) is The Shoulder of Mutton with Henry Harris's sign for carriage and cab hire; and (right) the distinctive vicarage.

17

Many people survived the bad old days, when milk was delivered, still warm from the cow, and ladled out from a pail into the customer's jug. Charles Mason of The Green, Barton, posed in front of the vicarage, was variously listed as dairyman or, more commonly, as cowkeeper. Soon after, the war memorial was to be added to this scene.

The Efflinch was common land following an enclosure act in 1812. In his *History of the Parish of Tatenhill* (1907) Sir Reginald Hardy of Dunstall Hall defines the name Efflinch as 'Heffalynge-lake; Heath-fallyng-lake'. This scene, *c.* 1911, shows, in the middle distance, the sign board of the former Junction Inn, a small public house recorded between 1851 and the 1920s, supposedly from a distant view of Wychnor rail junction rather than that with the main road.

DUNSTALL VILLAGE

F.W. Scarratt of Derby produced high quality and beautifully composed village scenes but sometimes could not resist including the light-weight motor cycle on which he travelled around. Without it this view could have been of the nineteenth century when Dunstall's stately church was founded (1853) by Charles, a son of Sir Richard Arkwright.

TATENHILL

Tatenhill nestled below Needwood Forest. The church, Early English though much restored, was, until 1881, the mother church for Barton. Overlooking the village is Battlestead Hill where historians believe the Britons fought early Angle invaders. After pre-war air displays it became the official RAF name (1940–45) for a relief landing ground (trainers), approached via Aviation Lane, Henhurst Hill, Burton.

Shakespeare's *Twelfth Night* was staged in the garden of 'The Croft', Mr F.A. Lowe's house at Tatenhill in June 1951. It was an idyllic setting but marred by the weather. F.A. Lowe was a well-known patron of the arts, following in the family tradition of sponsoring operatic productions, including *Cox and Box* at Tatenhill village hall in 1952. Burton Shakespeare Society players seen here are Frank Moorcroft, H. Wystan Hopcraft, and John Kelly.

Callingwood Hall photographed early this century. Around here Needwood Forest once came close to Burton. In the twelfth century Robert de Ferrers offered land to his bravest man-at-arms and it was Ralph de Knightley who chose what became the 'claimed wood', now Callingwood, appropriately called *Le Chaleng* in 1247. Nearby we now have Knightley Park and Woods and, little known and hidden away, there are traces of a small lost village.

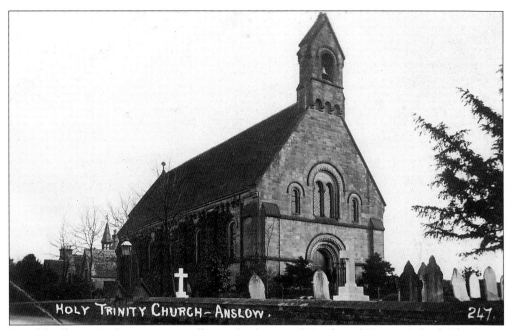

HOLY TRINITY CHURCH - ANSLOW. 247.

An old village, Anslow was originally on the fringes of Needwood Forest. Indeed, The Burnt Gate inn is a reminder of land cleared to become the 'Brende Woode' or Burnt Wood. Holy Trinity Church dates from c. 1850 and was once called Needwood Church. Its bell turret recalls traditions of a village curfew bell at Anslow to guide forest travellers or to summon the villagers – also suggested by the name of The Bell Inn.

Outwoods parish includes hills that form the western boundary of the Trent valley and from them one looks out over Burton, across the river and to Derbyshire beyond. Ninety years ago the lady in this artistic winter's day photograph took her binoculars with her to enjoy the panoramic view.

The Carnation House
Rangemore Gardens.

'Choice orchids, tropical flowers, and carnations as big as dahlias, filling the air with their perfumes. Rare exotics, rich foliage and delicate ferns were in magnificent profusion … creepers and hanging plants in every hue and variety depended from the roof', wrote Alfred Barnard, visiting Rangemore Hall in June 1887 during his tour of the Bass brewery while writing his book *Noted Breweries of Great Britain and Ireland*.

Primrose League Garden Party.
Rangemore Hall 27th June 1908

Domestic staff are attending to guests at a Primrose League Garden Party at Rangemore Hall on 27 June 1908. With East Staffordshire having many country houses it is hardly surprising that there were events on behalf of the League, its declared objects being 'the maintenance of religion, the estates of the realm and the imperial ascendancy of Great Britain.' These principles, advocated by Disraeli, prompted the League's foundation in 1883.

A close-up of the ageing King Edward VII at Rangemore in November 1907. His host, Lord Burton, was indisposed in London and plans for a house party were cancelled. The King stayed instead with Lord Shrewsbury at Ingestre, coming by car for a day's shooting, his personal pony travelling by train. It was the final royal occasion at Rangemore, Lord Burton dying in February 1909, the King in May 1910.

Byrkley, once a forest lodge, became another Bass family country house (demolished in 1952). In 1914 'Ethel' wrote sadly, 'This is one of the lakes … lots of little islands with daffs and primroses. You see the tower with the flag – my room is there and a huge clock chimes every quarter. I got into sad disgrace on Sunday – will tell you about it sometime.'

D. P. & S. CO.　　The Green, Newborough.　　D.

Robert de Ferrers established a twelfth-century settlement within Needwood Forest but his 'new borough' never greatly expanded, remaining today as Newborough village. It enjoyed some prosperity from linen bleaching when flax grew locally and later The Green became a milk market where dairies collected supplies from local farmers (see churns, centre). Facing, is the former post office and shop with the schoolmaster's house, left.

"THE GREEN" NEWBOROUGH

Looking back (1905) from the shop is The Red Lion and, right, the old forge (now Forge Cottage). One assumes an actual green here once, the tree and signpost as final reminders. Newborough church (to the right) was rebuilt and dedicated in 1901 and until the 1960s had graceful pinnacles at the base of the spire.

It was still mainly horse traffic when this photograph was taken. It is inscribed 'At the New Inn, Needwood' and the background survives. From here one can reflect on miles of straight roads through the Needwood countryside. These were surveyed by J.F. Calvert, Lord Vernon's agent, and built by Irish labourers. Mr Calvert is recorded as saying: 'I've travelled straight all my life and like others to do the same.'

This early motoring scene at Kingstanding recalls a former country house, the surrounding area becoming Tatenhill airfield (one part still used), built for the RAF in 1941, the B5234 being closed from The New Inn until the 1950s. The ladies wear fashionable motoring hats with veils, one of them taking over from the white-coated chauffeur (or just posing?).

Six Roads End near Draycott (Six Lanes, say locals, which probably they once were) presents quite a busy scene in this early Edwardian view when little greens still divided the ways from one another. The informative signpost listed three locations on each arm. Nearby is the woodyard of the Duchy of Lancaster, which owns an extensive area around here.

Hanbury village centre in this Edwardian scene also has an informative signpost outside the post office of that period. The youngsters (one with a hoop to bowl down the traffic-free lanes) no doubt attend the school seen in the background along with the church tower.

GEZ. H. M.   GESCH. G. E.

DIE KIRCHE ST. WERBURGH VON HANBURY

Hanbury church tower is a prominent landmark overlooking the Dove valley. The church is dedicated to St Werburgh, who established a nunnery here in the seventh century, and contains the oldest surviving alabaster effigy in the country (Sir John de Hanbury, dated 1303). The picture is something of a mystery. Undated, and acquired in a second-hand shop, it was understood to be the work of a German prisoner of war.

Hanbury's village pump as seen here in Martin's Lane has gone and houses occupy all the area to the right. Behind them is the rather less picturesque water tower. This view was taken about 1911 with the left-hand turn leading to the handsome church.

MARTIN'S LANE
HANBURY

Needwood Forest must once have had many little tree-lined ways like this, producing delightful scenes of light and shade. Leave the 'developed' right-hand side of Martin's Lane behind you and you reach this location, photographed in the 1930s but still little changed and opening out to give sweeping views.

A Victorian engraving by H. Warren shows Tutbury Castle on its hill overlooking the Dove valley. The horse-drawn wagon-way crossed the river from Tutbury cotton mill and was later replaced by a single line rail connection when it became Staton's plaster mill. That closed in 1968, the mill site becoming a picnic area although the disconnected railway line still remains crossing the river.

The Tutbury Horn, from a photograph in the reference library at Sheffield.

Possession of the ancient Tutbury Horn conferred on its holder certain posts and duties, including the offices of escheator and coroner throughout the Honour of Tutbury. Claimed as the symbol of their rights by the Agards, an old Staffordshire family (recalled by Agardsley Park), it later passed to the Stanhopes and then to the Greaves-Bagshawe family of Ford Hall, Derbyshire.

Two of East Staffordshire's greatest attractions are Tutbury Castle (admission a hundred years ago, one penny) and the Priory Church. The church's Norman west doorway (*c.* 1170) has elaborately decorated arches, the second from the inside being of local alabaster – its earliest known use in England.

Although inscribed 'The Meynell at Tutbury' (*c.* 1910) this is the Derbyshire side of the Dove. The house viewed sideways extreme right still stands on the main road in Hatton but this area adjoining Scropton Lane, where youngsters are watching the hunt assembling, has been either redeveloped or built over. The boy facing, third from left, is 'Our Jim' from 2 Castle Street.

Tutbury station closed in 1966 and was demolished but re-opened in 1990. This was it in its hey-day. The Great Northern Railway shared the station through working the Stafford–Uttoxeter Railway (opened 1867, closed 1951) trains running from Nottingham and Derby via Egginton and Bramshall junctions. The GNR also worked over the Burton-Tutbury line. Note milk churns along the west-bound platform.

North Staffordshire Railway 2–4–0 tank engine running as No. 2A in 1923 on the Burton–Tutbury 'Jinnie'. Built in 1890, originally numbered 2, it became LMS 1447 shortly after this photograph was taken. It was withdrawn and scrapped in 1930. It is approaching Tutbury station with Nestle's factory chimney prominent in the background.

The Staffordshire Knot had its beginnings in 1342 as a badge of the Earls of Stafford (later Dukes of Buckingham). This Stafford Knot was subsequently adopted by the town and county; by the military, constabulary and other bodies; and as a trademark and inn sign. The North Staffordshire Railway Company, which built most of the lines serving East Staffordshire, also appropriated it, as seen here, the system becoming affectionately and invariably known as 'The Knotty'. Their engines were crimson-lake, lined black, yellow and vermilion, with crimson-lake carriages.

ONE MILE
TO
TUTBURY.

Every Milestone near Tutbury brings us closer.

Many collectors have discovered the charm of sentimental Edwardian postcards. Usually a standard design was over-printed to serve a locality. This one, sent from Tutbury to Bramshall in 1909, says: 'Have enjoyed myself A1. Home to-morrow by the 9. 24. Wish I was just starting my holiday.' Perhaps the chosen card and message are the key to that enjoyment!

William Blood, fish, rabbit and poultry dealer of 3 Lower High Street, Tutbury, is delivering to the Foresters Arms, Scropton, on a frosty winter day. The village is just on the Derbyshire side of the Dove. A pair of lych gates lead to Scropton Church (rebuilt 1885–6), a few monuments surviving from an older building; and to a burial ground across the road.

Rolleston was another of the parks created out of Needwood Forest in early times. This is Rolleston Hall (largely demolished 1928), home of the Mosleys. Sir Oswald Mosley, 4th Bart., J.P. and Deputy Lieutenant of Staffordshire was High Sheriff in 1894. Here he is leaving for a ceremonial occasion accompanied by his chaplain, Canon Fielden, Rural Dean and Rector of St Mary's Rolleston.

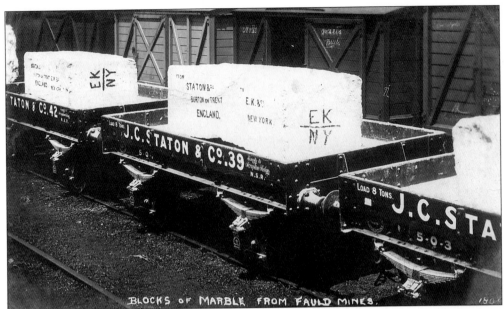

Scropton lost railway passenger service in 1872 but retained a goods yard from which Staton & Co. sent out alabaster blocks from their mine at Fauld. These are for export to New York *c.* 1906. From the numbers, Statons plainly had a substantial fleet of private owner wagons and operated a tramway down to the main line.

This picture looks up Draycott Cliff towards the Six Roads. The distant signpost marks the Uttoxeter turn (B5017). The highway was no doubt adequate for the traffic of 1906. Today these houses face a wide road with footpath, parking bays and constant traffic. The stack of building materials recalls how scaffolding was then erected using long wooden poles mounted in barrels of sand.

This Marchington photograph of The Square dates from ninety years ago and shows a pleasing grouping of architectural styles. The bay-windowed cottage with its three steps was the post office and the sender of this card comments: 'Our one shop is round the corner.' There was a public weighbridge near to the creeper-covered house.

Marchington Dramatic Society (founded 1922) presented the pantomime *Aladdin* in the village schoolroom for three nights in February 1925. In those days their publicity could include notice of a special late train running from Marchington to Uttoxeter at 10.00pm to cater for patrons.

A handsome trout caught in the Dove near Marchington in June 1912 by C. Hanson, junior. It was 22 inches long and weighed 4lb 12oz. Mr Hanson was secretary of Burton Angling Association and an enthusiastic naturalist. He lectured in the area on 'Fish Life as Revealed by the Camera'. Another study on local bird life listed the arrival of summer migrants from the 1890s to the 1930s.

Thomas Webb of Smallwood Manor near Uttoxeter was largely responsible for proposing and financing the building of St John's Church, Marchington Woodlands, which stands as a landmark on the fringes of Needwood Forest. Other local associations are that it was built by W. Evans of Ellastone (1858–9) using Hollington stone. Simple outside, it has the elaborate decorative interior favoured at this time.

One of the celebrated old oak trees of Needwood Forest photographed in 1905 with the Meynell Hunt posed in front. This was the Swilcar Lawn Oak, situated near Marchington Cliff. At five feet from the ground it had a girth at this time of 25 feet and was 60 feet high. Shaw in his *History of Staffordshire* called it 'the father of the forest' but, sadly, it no longer survives.

A notable tree in Bagot's Park near Abbots Bromley was the Beggars' Oak. People often visited it for a summer outing, as did these young ladies. Sixty feet high in the year 1907 and of great girth, some branches were given supports. By the late 1940s, however, these had gone, branches broke off, and this ancient forest giant quickly declined and is no more.

An Abbots Bromley procession celebrating King George V's Coronation in June 1911. St. Anne's School staged a patriotic parade headed by Britannia and attendants followed by groups whose banners proclaimed New Zealand, Historical Characters, British Flowers and British Possessions, among others, all elaborately costumed. The combined school (1921) of St Mary (1882) and St Anne (1874) is one of the oldest girls' public schools.

THE DINING HALL, ST. MARY'S, ABBOTS BROMLEY.

The young lady with a bad cold sending this view of St Mary's lamp-lit dining hall in 1904 was a keen postcard collector. 'I thought you would like this for your collection. I have 26 cards now. Hope you will send some more.' It was already a popular hobby, approved as being genteel and educational. Greenery relieves this formal lay-out with water bright to accompany the next meal!

40

Summer term 1911 has ended at St Anne's and carriers' carts and wagons are loading girls and their luggage for journeys to railway stations. Abbots Bromley never had a rail connection although there was a plan in 1863 for a branch line from Chartley to a terminus at Gapstile (between Harley Lane and Schoolhouse Lane). A later scheme was also withdrawn.

An early motoring scene in the square at Abbots Bromley alongside The Crown Hotel and the post office. The occasion could be electioneering. The Ford (left) has its registration number within the radiator grill. On the right is a Daimler (possibly the 1909 type 38 h.p. open tourer) displaying an early AA badge.

Most photographs of Abbots Bromley Horn Dance show it taking place in the village with an audience of visitors and tourists. By tradition the dance is also performed at several local venues and this 1928 photograph records the dance during a farm visit. On occasion they could be handicapped by the hospitality shown!

The late Tudor inn, The Goat's Head, in Abbots Bromley market square derives its name from the scarce breed of goats presented to the Bagots of Blithfield by Richard II (1377–99) The herd thrived on the estate until sold off in the late 1970s although the breed's continued preservation was ensured. This 1907 scene shows their enclosure among some of the notable old Bagot's Park oak trees.

42

Early photographs of Kingstone are elusive but this picture is taken from a Victorian glass negative. Kingstone Hall now has a somewhat altered aspect from this vantage point. Farm buildings remain alongside and the name of John Stonier who formerly farmed here is recalled by Stonier Drive which, with other housing, covers former farm land opposite St John's Church. This contains a memorial to the antiquary Sir Simon Degge, transferred from an earlier church.

Well known throughout the area, Major R.F. Ratcliff of the Bass, Ratcliff and Gretton brewery became Liberal Unionist MP for the Staffordshire Burton Division in 1900. He retained the seat at the elections of 1906, 1910 and 1911, remaining as MP until 1918. In 1914 he was one of the Company Commanders of the 6th Battalion, North Staffordshire Regiment.

No East Staffordshire album recalling past times would be complete without an old-fashioned farm scene. We were unable to trace the actual location but this evocative photograph is full of interest – the farm carts, the heavy horses wearing their ear covers, the milking stools on the cowshed window sills, the stackyard beyond with straw neatly cut out as required. One can almost conjure up the accompanying aromas!

Two
Wartime Recollections

Peace in South Africa.

THE LOXLEY CELEBRATION

in Commemoration of the Conclusion of Peace, will be held in the grounds of Highfields (the residence of Mrs. Sneyd Kynnersley), on Saturday, June 28th, 1902.

. . . PROGRAMME . . .

Dinner at 1=30 ;   Children's Tea at 3=30 ;   Ladies' Tea at 4=30.

Songs by the Bramshall Glee Party.

Old English Sports, Cricket and Lawn Tennis, Punch and Judy, Ventriloquism.   Dancing at 6.   Rocester Brass Band.

Mr. *Gallimore Junr*

At Highfields, Uttoxeter, celebrations were held on 28 June 1902 to celebrate peace in South Africa (end of the Boer War, 1899–1902). The grounds were open to all and this surviving invitation card lists the day's programme, events and performers. A later occupant of Highfields was Judge Ruegg K.C. Now much altered, it is a home for the elderly.

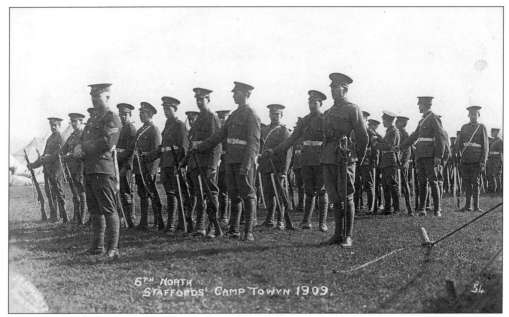

Before the First World War (1914–18), Uttoxeter's territorials included a detachment of the 6th Battalion, North Staffordshire Regiment, based at the drill hall under Lieutenants H.B. and D.J. Bamford. The company drill instructor was Sergeant G.J. Brown. There were annual battalion training camps such as Towyn, 1909. Many of these men were among the first into action in 1914.

Simnett and Abrahams of Burton photographed many military scenes both locally and in camps elsewhere. Such scenes by McCann of Uttoxeter are scarce but here is an informal shot of signallers (location unknown). In spite of advances in technology telescopes and mirrors (also lamps) still remained part of an army signaller's training during the Second World War.

Officers a Men of C Sq. S.Y. for Foreign Service.

The Staffordshire Volunteer Cavalry (Yeomanry), formed in 1794, became the Queen's Own Royal Regiment in 1838. The Anglesey (Burton) Troop and the Uttoxeter Troop became part of the territorial army early this century. In 1914 Major H.A. Clowes commanded 'C' squadron with Major G.P. Heywood (of Doveleys, Denstone), Second-in-Command. These Staffordshire volunteers were quickly mobilised when war broke out.

BELGIAN REFUGEES AT MARCHINGTON UTTOXETER

Early in the First World War, refugees from Belgium were brought to East Staffordshire, Burton being the main reception area and the mayor establishing a Belgian War Relief Fund. Photographic records are scarce but McCann of Uttoxeter recorded some Belgian families apparently accommodated in the Marchington area. The windows of seventeenth-century Marchington Hall form the background for this group.

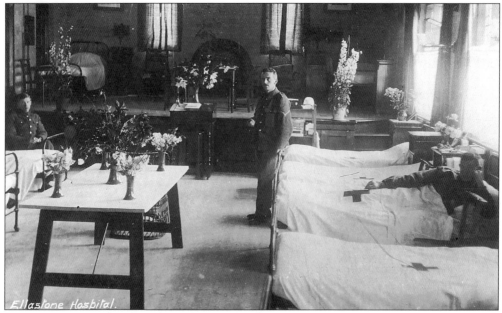

Ellastone Hospital.

After money was raised by public subscription Ellastone Church Hall and Reading Room was opened in 1911 but soon had to be utilised for other purposes when the Red Cross adapted it as a small hospital ward in the First World War. The soldier standing by his bed is Lance-Corporal G. Williams of the 2nd Manchester Regiment.

Christmas Greetings
to the LAND ARMY 1918

YOUR LANTERN TO THE STABLE BRING,
THE BEASTS ARE COLD, THE NIGHT IS WILD;
YET KNOW A GREATER LIGHT IS HERE,
WHOSE LANTERN IS THE HOLY CHILD.

In both world wars women took over jobs normally done by men and members of the Women's Land Army worked on local farms. Although the war had finally finished by Christmas 1918, men had not yet returned in great numbers and this greetings card was sent by a local land girl who later became a farmer's wife.

This Abbots Bromley procession passes a poster announcing Peace Celebrations (First World War). The girls display a wide range of costumes as they follow a 'Pied Piper'. The scene shows the hexagonal butter cross (seventeenth century) and the timber-framed Goat's Head Inn of the late sixteenth century. The state of the roadway suggests that cars are still few and far between.

In 1921, a lych gate to St Michael's Church, Rocester, was dedicated as the war memorial. Tom Gaunt, later a church warden, recalled his nervousness as a youngster when providing a muffled drum roll as the band played the 'Dead March' from *Saul*, the vicar unobtrusively indicating louder or softer. The shaft of a thirteenth-century cross is in the churchyard and nearby earthworks mark the site of Rocester Abbey (*c.* 1146).

Uttoxeter war memorial was unveiled on a wet 11 November 1928. Forty-five Second World War (1939–45) names were later added to four times that number for the First World War. The ceremony over, we see a damp, deserted Market Place and the shops of Edwin Roberts, outfitter; a branch of Star Tea Company; and Orme's furnishing department.

A photograph recalling early days of the Home Guard in the Rocester area. On 14 May 1940 the formation of a new home defence force was announced – Local Defence Volunteers. On 23 July the name was changed to the Home Guard which quickly became a well-trained and efficient force. This picture precedes the full issue of uniforms and weapons, most of them being double-barrelled shotguns.

Longcroft Hall near Yoxall was demolished in 1952 but during the Second World War was utilised as a Home Guard Training Centre, many local men attending courses here. In 1941 Tutbury, Alrewas and Marchington battalions amalgamated with Burton to produce a force of some 2,500 men. This view shows the hall and 'E' company (commanded by Major W.J. Ison, MSM) on parade during a training exercise.

In 1940 Uttoxeter became a reception area for evacuees from Ramsgate, among them Mrs Doris Hamlin and two small sons, Lionel and David, photographed here in 1942 on the Recreation Ground. After sharing a bungalow near the dairy, Mrs Hamlin moved into rooms over Cope's butcher's shop in the Market Place, furnished only with the barest necessities. She still recalls the great kindness and help promptly received from Uttoxeter people – and the minor sensation when her husband came on leave from the Navy and brought a banana!

A peaceful 1930s scene when Stephen Saffron was landlord of Hanbury's local pub. Its sign carries no name but it was *Directory*-listed as The Fighting Cock. Just after 11.00am on 27 November 1944, a huge underground bomb store near Fauld exploded. Seventy-three people were killed and the inn so badly damaged it had to be rebuilt. The massive crater remains as a memorial and war grave while the new Cock Inn records inside other aspects of Britain's biggest explosion.

Looking along Carter Street, Uttoxter, from the GPO, the low seventeenth-century building, right, is now Uttoxeter Heritage Centre. It was once the home of Francis Redfern, the local historian. We include this 1940s scene here, however, because of the Pool Petrol pump, all petroleum trade names being in abeyance during the war.

Uttoxeter Dramatic Society presented Terence Rattigan's popular war-time play *Flare Path* at the Town Hall in November 1950. Set in the lounge of a Lincolnshire hotel surrounded by airfields, the programme called it a reminder of recent times and the trials and triumphs of 'those who served'. Produced by Mary Bagshaw, the cast list included Madeleine Dale, H.G. Sadler, Eva Ohm, Thomas Blakey, John Lee, Harold Wilks, Robert Weston, Doreen Baker, Marjorie Tipper, Lelise Newbold, and John Steventon.

Three
Around Uttoxeter

A familiar sight in East Staffordshire, Stevenson's buses first ran from Uttoxeter to Burton on 11 September 1926 using a 26-seater Reo. In spite of a fire at Spath garage in 1930, services expanded and double deckers appeared in 1946. This 1947 acquisition, a 1930 Leyland Titan, was obtained from Paisley, hence its Scottish registration GE 7222. It ran locally until withdrawn in 1954. Spath, incidentally, saw the installation of Britain's first automatic railway level crossing in February 1961.

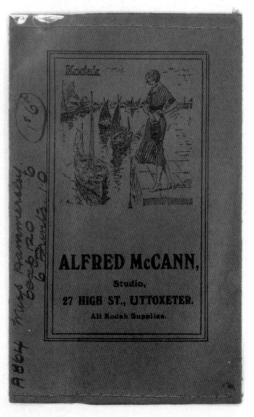

Uttoxeter's leading photographer Alfred
McCann produced carte de visite photographs in pre-postcard days. Here, a
typical late Victorian child study. The
highly decorative back on an earlier example is inscribed E. McCann. Edward
McCann, in the 1870s, was also Assistant
Overseer and Collector of Poor Rates. On
Alfred's later folder is Miss Hammers-
ley's bill for 6 exposures and 6 prints
at 7½ pence in to-day's money.

An aerial view showing the south side of Uttoxeter dominated by the original Bamford's Leighton Ironworks, established in 1871, later covering 24 acres and employing hundreds of workers before it finally closed down. A guidebook commented: 'Uttoxeter's chief trade is dairy produce but recently factories for agricultural implements and corset-making (in the old canal warehouse) have given employment to many hands.' Contrasting types of precision work!

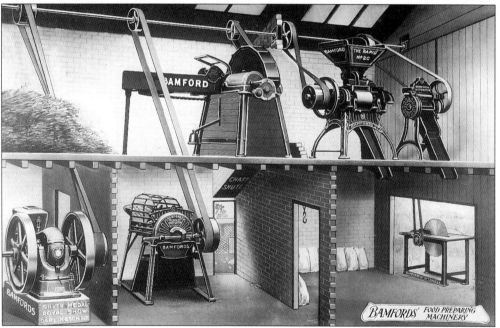

A Bamford's publicity postcard showing machinery for producing animal feeds. The engine driving the belts records a silver medal awarded at the 1920 Royal Show in Darlington. These are products from the Leighton Ironworks, whose trade marks included 'Royal' and 'Lion' haymaking equipment and 'Clipper' and 'Perfect' food producing machines, Royal Show winners as early as 1905.

Christmas publicity 1904 for Ormes of Uttoxeter. These specially printed postcards went out in November to encourage early Christmas shopping. This card shows a good example of the Uttoxeter 'Duplex' postmark with the local post office number 827, a Victorian cancellation sometimes continuing in use until early this century. Did Ormes study the popular 'Language of Stamps' of the day? Its position, face downwards, signified 'Answer at once'.

Orme's Christmas publicity was not without its humour, as appears here, and this is also an example of the work of Lawson Wood, a well-known postcard artist, as well as being a leading illustrator for magazines, theatrical posters, etc.

A close-up of a shop usually only a name in the background of Market Place scenes. In the 1890s Mrs Elizabeth Furbank was established here requesting 'the favor [sic] of a visit' to view French and English millinery but by 1912 the premises had become those of E.S. Wilks & Son, drapers. Note the traditional front parlour aspidistra in the upper window.

Hankinsons (c. 1903), previously Johnsons, was started in 1790 by Thomas Woolrich. Mr Hankinson advertised 'two important principles – all drugs must be absolutely pure; and prices charged must be the lowest possible.' He was also noted for animal medicines 'handed down with the business.' Sparklet syphons form his pavement display. In stock are Kodak box cameras, invented with roll films in 1888. Solio P.O.P. is printing out paper for photography.

SHAKE OFF WINTER!

PARKER'S SARSAPARILLA COMP.

is more than a Sarsaparilla Extract.

It is a gentle, natural laxative for the bowels and liver; a diuretic for the Kidneys—by which means the blood is purified; an alterative for excretions—**its Most Noticeable Effect is seen on the Complexion, but the Real Effect is seen throughout the Body;** a Tonic for the secretions—shows benefit quickest in sections of the stomach, stimulating the gastric and other juices.

This is a Splendid Medicine for this time of the year.

2s. 9d. bottles for **2s. 3d.**, **4s. 6d.** bottles for **3s. 9d.**

One Bottle will put the System in Condition.

A. PARKER,

Chemist,

UTTOXETER.

PARKER'S VIGOR TONIC

. . . is for Weak People . . .

Weak from sickness, old age, overwork, worry, or indulgence.

This Elixir is thoroughly professional, just such as is prescribed constantly by careful physicians. **Exceedingly Strengthening. Agrees with every stomach. Pleasant.**

ONE SHILLING A BOTTLE.

PRINTED BY P. J. DAMS, UTTOXETER.

Another High Street chemist, Alfred Parker, produced this advertising handbill around 1890 when a local directory also listed him as a dentist. The poster is a good example of the practice of Victorian printers using as many different types and sizes of print as possible.

COLIC DRINK

DIRECTIONS.—Give this Mixture immediately the animal is observed to be in pain, and another dose in an hour if no relief is obtained. For animals over six and under twelve months old, give half the above quantity.

DIET.—After administering this Medicine, allow some warm sloppy Bran Mashes and water with the chill off.

ALFRED PARKER,
DISPENSING CHEMIST
HIGH STREET, UTTOXETER.

After collecting your own remedy from Alfred Parker you could also obtain a suitable medicine for your horse – taking care, of course, not to get your bottles mixed! This is a gummed label for sticking on the horse-medicine bottle.

Although titled 'Staff of Uttoxeter District Prudential Assurance Co.', this large, elegant group rather suggests a gathering of agents and wives for a social occasion. One often hears reference to 'The man from the Pru' and he was certainly involved in every description of business from small householders to major firms, with the company's invested funds advertised, even in 1905, as exceeding £77 million.

A view across Uttoxeter Market Place *c.* 1906. At the far end was Albert Perry (military and livery tailor), Samuel Bullar (hairdresser, later Dales), Phillips (Plumbers, painters and glaziers) and the Old Talbot Inn, then prominently advertising Peter Walker's ales and stout. To the right we see Proctors (clothiers), Hunters the Teamen Limited, and Hall's Travel Bureau.

The Peter Walker breweries were at Warrington and Burton and they had an agency and depot in Carter Street for many years. This publicity card for their lager beer played on the competition between British and German lagers. Says the German to John Bull: 'Hoch! yours was der best.'

Hunters were early pioneers in giving free stamps with purchases. This book needed filling with 390 of their little red coupons to be worth 10p in today's money.

M.V. STAFFORDSHIRE.

Adjoining Hunters, Hall & Son were official steamship, tourist, shipping and insurance agents with special offers encouraging emigration to the British Colonies. A later Bibby Line publicity postcard, after Halls had moved to High Street, showed the motor vessel *Staffordshire*. Halls have returned to the Market Place but the emphasis today is on bus, rail, air and car ferry travel for holidays.

The Bank House, now a restaurant and hotel, is so called because Thomas Hart established Uttoxeter's first bank here in the eighteenth century. The old safe still exists and another feature is a fine unsupported spiral staircase. Around 1904, W. Hall of Widnes photographed the magnificent wisteria trained across the front, designating his view as 'One of Uttoxeter's Beauty Spots'.

This Elizabethan bed was among items auctioned at Uttoxeter Town Hall in March 1908 following 'instructions from several gentlemen who are leaving the town.' In spite of postcard publicity and display at Gerrard's antique shop in High Street, it seems to have attracted limited interest and we could find no record of the price fetched or where it went. In today's *Antiques Roadshow* it would no doubt attract more enthusiasm!

Most Uttoxeter photographs were taken by McCann but this portrait is by A.C. Glover who had a stationer's shop in High Street. The unknown lady was no doubt proud of her hat which, as a fashion writer describes, would be 'balanced carefully on the pinned-up hair, tilted over the brow and skewered into place with steel hatpins ten inches long.'

George Richardson, wheelwright, had premises in Bradley Street by 1835 and later at Heath. This publicity card shows Richardsons established as coach builders at the Wharf Carriage Works in Park Street and displaying a wide range of vehicles. They were also an agency for selling and repairing Meteor and Rover cycles.

Park Street in the early 1920s shows Richardsons moving with the times, their sign now proclaiming: Coach and Motor Works, Garage and Pit. It continues as a garage in the original premises, the upper floor little altered outwardly. The sedate corner house has now acquired a shop window.

A rickshaw built by Richardsons for the Parish Church bazaar of 1905. The County Museum at Shugborough Hall has displayed a similar model with details about the firm, including the surprising information that they exported rickshaws to Shanghai.

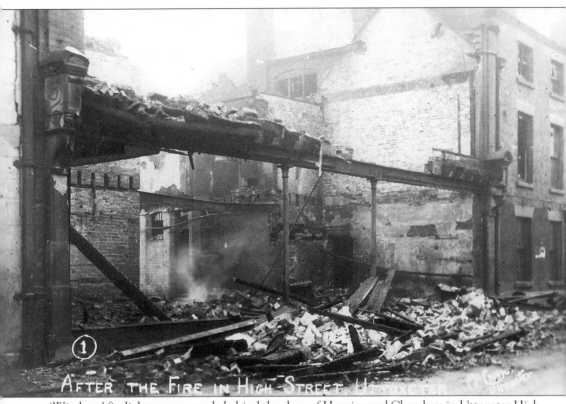

AFTER THE FIRE IN HIGH STREET UTTOXETER

'Witchem' firelighters were made behind the shop of Huggins and Chambers in Uttoxeter High Street. The premises were gutted when fire broke out at 6.00am on Thursday 11 November 1909. An employee was cleaning out fires under coppers where chemicals were heated when live coals fell on waste materials and the blaze quickly assumed serious proportions. The shop itself supplied petrol, oil, paraffin, tyres and other inflammable items – a set-up that sounds like a modern safety inspector's nightmare. There was limited water supply until the steam fire engine arrived under Captain Hollins – the local paper claimed in twenty minutes; another newspaper about an hour before the steamer 'got going'. These photographs show the destruction. Adjoining properties were damaged but fortunately there was no wind although it took several hours to contain and finally extinguish the fire.

Opposite: One can imagine a possible comment from one of these firemen that 'Witchem' firelighters had at least proved their efficiency.

AFTER THE FIRE AT THE 'WITCHEM' FIRELIGHTE'
WORKS UTTOXETER 2. McCANN. P6

Uttoxeter had one of the earliest National Schools to be established. It expanded quickly and the Bradley Street Centre is all that now remains of an 1855 building (enlarged 1893) which catered for generations of local children. These girl pupils were photographed in the late 1890s when the school had 150 boys (Master, George Tortoishell), 110 girls (Mistress, Miss H.M. Gee) and 150 infants (Mistress, Miss M. Smith).

St Joseph's Catholic School at Mount Pleasant opened in 1930, moving from the original buildings of 1873 at the rear of the Catholic Church in Balance Street. This group is in the old school yard early this century when Christine Dale and Monica Morris were young teachers. There is no information about the performance but the three bears are prominent in very convincing costumes.

An Edwardian view of Dove Bank where Derby Road approaches Uttoxeter from Dove Bridge. Around the distant bend was a level crossing for the Churnet railway and the lines can just be seen. Uttoxeter once had three stations, one at the end of this view by the crossing, named Dove Bank, the others being Bridge Street and Junction Station.

Uttoxeter's original three separate stations were combined in this new structure of 1881. An overbridge replaced Bridge Street level crossing and platforms were connected by the covered footbridge. This view shows a large station staff and a train at the Churnet line platform with North Staffordshire tank engine No. 40, also of 1881 which, as LMS 1456, worked until 1932; the main line platform for Derby to the right.

CARTER STREET, UTTOXETER

The accompanying message makes this Carter Street scene of special interest. 'St. Mary's Guest House [Home of Rest: Matron, Mrs Berridge] is just off the edge of the picture facing the White Hart. Notice the stylish vehicle which is the only public omnibus. It belongs to the hotel and has to be ordered in advance, the charge being sixpence per head, luggage included, to the station. At present the only horse has damaged himself so the bus is getting a rest too.' The terra cotta building, right, is the GPO. The large board above the White Hart balcony reads: 'Headquarters of the Automobile Club of Great Britain and Ireland' which became the RAC in 1907.

The Manor House, Uttoxeter, early this century when it was the residence of His Honor, Judge Alfred Henry Ruegg KC, JP (County Court Judge of North Staffordshire and Joint Judge of Birmingham). In this photograph the coach is occupied by Miss Ruegg, the Judge's sister, and driven by his coachman, George Bates. Subsequently the Judge moved to Highfields.

The Judge's vehicles over the years reflect trends and changes in the local traffic scene. By the early 1920s George Bates has become chauffeur instead of coachman but this model follows in the coach tradition with its fold-down hood. Here, Miss Ruegg, her sister and friends are probably visiting Rudyard Lake, an immensely popular tourist venue at this time.

Around 1930 the Judge was using this more sedate saloon car though it still had the facility for lowering the hood over the rear passenger seat. George Bates, who lived at Dove Bank, remained in demand as a coachman, however, driving the carriage for the Uttoxeter Carnival Queen.

These cheerful Uttoxeter motor cyclists of 1919, recently returned from war service, were Frank Dale, astride the Triumph combination, with his brother, Charles, still nursing a war wound, in the wicker-work sidecar. The family lived in Balance Street. Frank had a long career at Pakemans, grocers, at 17 Market Place while Charles ran a hairdressing business for many years at No. 3, once the Spread Eagle public house.

Staffordshire Farmers' Association.

UTTOXETER BRANCH.

A **General Meeting** of Members of the above will be held at the **"Black Swan"** Inn on **Wednesday next,** February 19th, 1902, at 2 o'clock.

AGENDA :

To consider the Price of Milk for the ensuing Season.

Other Business.

Yours faithfully,

G. FLETCHER BAGSHAW,

Hon. Secretary.

The important local issue of milk prices formed the agenda for this 1902 meeting at The Black Swan, Market Street. This notice went to E.S. Fletcher who was the last manager of the Burton, Uttoxeter and Ashbourne Union Bank (1839) in Carter Street, prior to its acquisition by Lloyds Bank on 1 January 1899. The meeting unanimously agreed wholesale prices for milk sent to London as 8p per gallon in winter (1s 8d), reducing in summer.

A scene from the days of the milk pail, milking stool and milkmaid and a twice-daily chore on the many dairy farms within our area. John Leland's Itinerary entry (c. 1540) says: 'The inhabitants [of Uttoxeter] are graziers because there are marvellous pasture grounds beside the Dove.' Milking competitions such as this were a feature of local shows.

Over one hundred years ago there was an active Uttoxeter Amateur Swimming Club with a pavilion on the banks of the Dove. Contests and exhibitions were popular, big crowds collecting to watch, as here in 1908, with seating provided for the ladies, but subsequently these events were abandoned on safety grounds.

Swimming Pool in Recreation Ground, Uttoxeter.

Land for Uttoxeter Recreation Ground was given by Mr C.H. Elkes and it was formally opened during the first Annual Carnival in 1925. Swimming again became popular locally when, in 1930, this open air bath was completed. It had basic accommodation plus the odd lifebelt. The brook water supply, however, was subsequently condemned, leading to closure and replacement, firstly by the Lido and now by today's Leisure Centre pool.

McCann faithfully recorded the casts of Uttoxeter Operatic Society's productions performed at the Town Hall. Often they chose the more familiar Gilbert and Sullivan comic operas (*The Mikado*, 1904, repeated in 1908); but in April 1906 the Society presented one of the earliest and less well-known works, *The Sorcerer*, first staged in 1877 before the start of the famous Savoy seasons.

Uttoxeter Swifts F.C., 1903/4, probably had a fixture list dictated by ease and cost of travelling. When Uttoxeter Oldfields F.C. applied to join Burton District Association for 1907/8 they were only accepted after undertaking to pay half the train fares of opposition players travelling to Uttoxeter. Oldfields finished second to Tutbury Town in Division I, scoring 128 goals in 28 matches, then winning without a defeat in 1908/9. Uttoxeter St Mary's F.C. played in Division II.

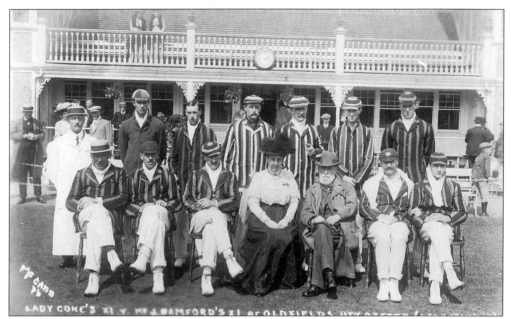

John Bamford laid out the splendid Oldfields sports ground and entertained Australian, South African, and West Indies cricket teams in matches against guest elevens which would include test and county players. In July 1910 distinguished amateurs and professionals assembled for Lady Coke's XI to meet Mr John Bamford's XI over two days, the England players including the Hon. F.S. Jackson, R.E. Foster, and Sidney Barnes, who took ten wickets.

This smart group is a joint gathering of Boy Scouts from Uttoxeter and Rocester. Founded in 1908 by Baden Powell, the Scout movement quickly achieved great popularity. The year is 1912 and one wonders how many of the older lads here were soon called upon to face a sterner challenge when war broke out in 1914.

The Earl of Meath originated Empire Day, celebrated from 1904, on 24 May, the anniversary of Queen Victoria's birthday. It was widely commemorated in schools and the Junior Imperial and Constitutional League was a further expression of support for Empire ideals. It was also active socially and this 1923 photograph shows their fancy dress dance at Uttoxeter Town Hall.

With the opening of a £2 million grandstand by Prince Edward on 1 October 1994, the old look of Uttoxeter Racecourse has become part of the past. This permanent course for National Hunt racing was established in 1908 by the Urban District Council but there are records of race meetings in Uttoxeter from the early eighteenth century including a sweepstake for 100 guineas staged in 1774.

The A50 with no traffic in sight and little talk yet of by-passes. The view looks into Derbyshire from the old Dove Bridge with its recesses for pedestrians. The former toll house is on the left. The Newcastle-Derby road was turnpiked in 1759, Uttoxeter soon becoming a coaching centre supplying horses for several services, the White Hart being the principal coaching inn.

Close to Uttoxeter but across the Dove in Derbyshire, Doveridge's *Domesday* name of 'Dubrige' suggests it should be Dovebridge. The 'Jubilee Well' is now closed up and has become an attractive ornamental feature. The houses, left, remain little altered but the fields opposite have been built on.

DOVERIDGE, Derbyshire.

Valuable Freehold ACCOMMODATION LAND, COTTAGES & GARDENS.

TO be SOLD by AUCTION by Messrs. HARDY & HARDY, at the "Cross Keys" Hotel, Uttoxeter, on Wednesday, the 15th day of May, 1901, at 2 for 3 o'clock in the afternoon, and subject to Conditions of Sale—

Lot 1
All that Freehold DWELLING-HOUSE with Outbuildings comprising Tying for 5 cows, Chophouse, Piggeries, &c., together with the Garden and CLOSE of Fine Old TURF LAND adjoining thereto situate in Lower Street, Doveridge, and containing by Ordnance Survey 2a. 2r. 7p., and now in the occupation of Mr. W. Kirkland.

Lot 2
All that CLOSE of Freehold Rich Old Turf Accommodation LAND (part of which has been recently planted) situate at Doveridge aforesaid, having extensive frontages to Sand Lane and the main road, containing 1a. 3r. 6p., and now in the occupation of Mr. Robinson.

Lot 3
All that Freehold Plot of GARDEN GROUND adjoining the last lot, and situate opposite the Post Office at Doveridge, now used as an Allotment Ground, containing 1815 square yards or thereabouts.

Lot 4
All those Two Freehold CLOSES of Fine Old Turf LAND, situate at Doveridge aforesaid, known as "The Upfields," containing by Ordnance Survey 19a. 1r. 4p., and now in the occupation of Mr. Isaac Thompson as yearly tenant. This Land is in good heart and condition and well watered.

Lot 5
All that Freehold Plot of GARDEN GROUND situate at the corner of Baker's Lane, Doveridge, containing 817 square yards, and now in the occupation of Mr. S. Sturgess.

Lot 6.
All those Four Freehold COTTAGES and Gardens situate in Sand Lane, Doveridge, now in the respective occupations of G. Bradbury, J. Harris, Wm. Gaunt and W Mosely. These Cottages always command good tenants.

Lot 7.
All those Six Freehold COTTAGES and Gardens adjoining the last lot and situate in the centre of the village of Doveridge, now in the occupation of Wilshaw. Bradbury, A. Smith and others.

Lot 8.
All those Two Freehold COTTAGES and Gardens situate near the last lot, and adjoining the Village Reading-Room and Recreation Ground, now in the occupation of A. Wainwright and Arthur Smith.

Lot 9.
All that Freehold CLOSE of Fine Old Turf Meadow LAND, known as "Hay Meadow," situate near the Holt Wood Farm, numbered 731 on the Ordnance Survey Plan containing 4a. 0r. 39p. or thereabouts and now in the occupation of Mr. John Townsend.

Lot 10.
All those Three Freehold COTTAGES and Gardens situate at Doveridge, adjoining Lot 2, and now void.

Lot 11.
All that Freehold MESSUAGE formerly used as a Toll House, and situate by the main road near the Dove Bridge, now in the occupation of Hy. Sheppard.

To view the Properties, apply to the respective Tenants, and for further information and to view Plan, apply to the AUCTIONEERS, Uttoxeter and Ashbourne; or to

Mr. C. H. COWLISHAW,
Solicitor, Uttoxeter

An unusual item to intrigue present-day residents of Doveridge. This circular announced the sale of eleven lots of property in 1901 at The Cross Keys Hotel, Uttoxeter. Dating from 1697, this building has now become the offices of Bagshaws, Estate Agents, who conducted the auction. The lots were disposed of as follows: (1) Withdrawn at £300; (2) £255; (3) £100; (4) £1200; (5) £37; (6) £300; (7) Withdrawn at £400; (8) £185; (9) £245; (10) £150; (11) £121 (see picture on left).

The writer of this postcard has enjoyed a day's hunting with the Meynell, here seen assembling at Doveridge Hall, at this time (1910) the residence of Lord Waterpark. The house was built in 1769 by Edward Stevens for Sir Henry Cavendish with the main frontage looking out across the Dove valley. It was demolished in 1938.

Edwardian Bramshall with villagers watching a meet of the Meynell Hunt. These houses remain though with various alterations while new properties have appeared, right, where the former smithy has become the post office. At this time letters were delivered from Uttoxeter, the nearest money order and telegraph office, and a wall letter-box was cleared once daily. A change for the worse, say villagers, is today's road traffic.

84

Foliage now hides much of this view of Lower Leigh. Chestnut Cottage (right) was the Police House next to the Railway Inn and shop. The inn is now a residence, timber facing no longer visible but still displaying S. Sherratt's 1751 inscription: 'Walk in my friend and drink with me; Here's ALE as good as e'er you see … '. Moorhouse Farm and Rose Cottage remain but the green has lost its working smithy.

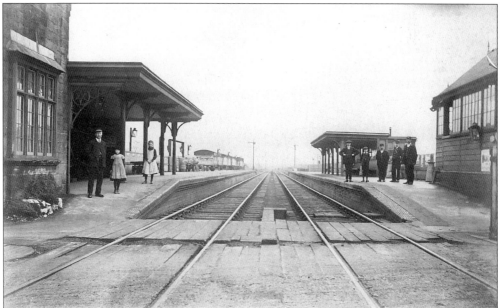

The former Railway Inn at Leigh was obviously renamed after 1848 when the Stoke–Uttoxeter line opened with Leigh station built nearby. It survived until 1966 although the lines and level crossing remain. This is a typical North Staffordshire country station with the station master and daughters a little aloof from the other members of staff (c. 1910). Milk churns and vans are prominent but station name boards seem to have been temporarily removed.

Pub, chapel and church are all in view looking up Stramshall's main street *c.* 1904. The Methodist Chapel was then new, the original of 1841 being rebuilt in 1899. £1,200 was raised to build the church in 1850–52, the architect being Thomas Fradgley who designed Uttoxeter Town Hall. At The Hare and Hounds father and son – both named Thomas Griffin – were, in turn, innkeepers from the 1890s until the 1930s.

This picture was sent with best wishes for Christmas 1927 and may not have been inappropriate in cattle country, since it probably displays a prize Christmas bullock. Our information suggests that the photograph was taken at Stramshall.

Four
A Literary Interlude

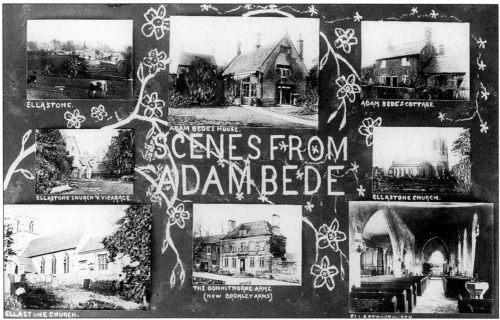

Television has created revived interest in George Eliot's novels, particularly *Adam Bede*, but this multi-view postcard by R & R Bull of Ashbourne dates from c. 1904. Although George Eliot (Mary Ann Evans 1819–1881) was born near Nuneaton, her father came from Roston near Norbury (top right picture) and he was her original for Adam. The other scenes concentrate on Ellastone, featured in her book as Heyslope, with The Bromley Arms becoming The Donnithorne Arms. Norbury is Norbourne; Ashbourne is Oakbourne; Dovedale becomes Eagledale; while Staffordshire and Derbyshire are Loamshire and Stonyshire.

Dr. Johnson Bas-relief.   Uttoxeter.

Visitors on a literary trail will want to look at the Dr Johnson bas-relief on the conduit in Uttoxeter market place. Copied from a statue in Lichfield Cathedral, it shows Johnson's act of penance when an elderly man because, as a youth, 'I refused to attend my father to Uttoxeter market.'

'Lucy has read ... Tom Moore all through, every word ... I believe she knows most of Tom Moore by heart', writes Anthony Trollope in one of his Barset novels (1867). Although popular into this century, few people probably read or know Tom Moore's poems today. The stone cottage at Mayfield, where he spent some years writing, became a farm but was a subject for Edwardian postcards.

By 1832 Holly Bush Hall, Newborough, was 'an elegant, comfortable residence' but earlier F.N.C. Mundy of Markeaton had rented it as a hunting lodge. It inspired his poem *The Fall of Needwood* following disafforestation:

> How chang'd! those oaks that tower'd so high,
> Dismember'd, stript, extended lie;
> On the stain'd turf their wrecks are pil'd;
> Where thousand summers bask'd and smiled
> In smouldering heaps their limbs consume,
> The dark smoke marks their casual tomb.

Wootton Hall, demolished c. 1935, was the home of the Davenports. An earlier house became the temporary residence in 1766–7 of the French philosopher Jean Jacques Rousseau. There he wrote his *Confessions*, his last work. He chose Wootton for peace and seclusion (yearly rental £30), wrote, studied botany, and visited Bernard Granville at Calwich Abbey nearby, but his eccentricities verged on madness and he suddenly fled, convinced his cook was poisoning him.

Originally one of the old Needwood Forest lodges, this later mansion at Yoxall has also been demolished. One occupier was Thomas Gisborne, writer and poet, and friend of William Wilberforce who, with Gisborne, wrote an anti-slavery report here. Also from Yoxall came Thomas Astle (born 1735), a scholar and collector of noted Medieval manuscripts, now in the British Museum.

This lodge at an entrance to Bagot's Park, known as the Goat House, was built in 1835. The postcard (c. 1903) carries the message: 'Goats' heads carved by your grandfather' but unfortunately it is not addressed. The lodge is now incorporated into the private residence of the naturalist and writer Phil Drabble, whose efforts have created a nature reserve here and helped to conserve the surrounding area.

We are told that the library at Rangemore Hall, with its deep recessed windows, was much favoured by visitors providing alcoves overlooking the gardens and ideal for correspondence or playing games. King Edward VII, an ardent bridge player, was partnered here and at other country houses by Lady Burton's sister, Miss Jane Thornewill, considered to be 'the best woman bridge player in England.'

Stanton, up on the Weaver hills, was the birth place of Gilbert Sheldon, who became Archbishop of Canterbury in the reign of Charles II. He asked Sir Christopher Wren to design a building to serve as a University Theatre for Oxford and also to accommodate the University Press, providing the money for its erection, 1664–9. His arms appear over the entrance. (See page 120)

In addition to his legal duties Judge Ruegg, when resident at Highfields, Uttoxeter, wrote a series of novels in the 1920s set within the county. A publicity postcard recommended his books as follows: 'Staffordshire is not a county that has figured much in fiction but His Honor, Judge Ruegg, has introduced it to us in his capably written novels .... Lovers of the wild moorlands of Staffordshire should read *John Clutterbuck*, *A Staffordshire Knot*, *Flash: A Moorland Mystery*; and *David Betterton*.

The dust cover of Judge Ruegg's *A Staffordshire Knot*. It was published in 1926 but is essentially a late Victorian melodrama. It is, nevertheless, what used to be called 'a good yarn' with, perhaps predictably, its best scenes in the court sequences that provide the climax, including a description of formalities at the commencement of the Staffordshire Assizes.

Staffs. Harry Lauder.
over £10,000 for Charities.

A popular entertainer all around the county during and after the First World War was 'Staffordshire's Harry Lauder' – Wilmot Martin. Born near Stafford in 1874 he farmed at Gratwich near Uttoxeter around the turn of the century (also forming the cricket club). Moving to Hixon in 1906, he began organising concert parties and created his own act singing Harry Lauder songs. His performances raised over £10,000 for the war effort and for charities. He told his own story in *A Minstrel in Staffordshire*.

Five

To Rocester
and the Weaver Hills

Dominant at Rocester now are the landscaped grounds and lakes surrounding the JCB Excavator factory, originating in 1950 when J.C. Bamford took over a former cheese factory. Gone are the Redhill Bank Brickworks, seen here *c.* 1903, railway station (off right), The Railway Inn and much else, cleared for the company's rapid expansion. Ruined Woodseat Hall nearby was then the residence of John Fitzherbert Campbell, Lord of the Manor.

This multi-view collection of scenes around Rocester about 1905 was produced for Christmas by W.H. Hall, a photographer from Widnes. Left: fishing below the Dove weir; and all the inhabitants of Dove Lane popping out of their houses. Centre is Rocester Church with, right, a

St Greetings from Rocester.

distant view of the mill and the Infant School scholars. They include little Irene Moss whose brother Jack, we are told, is just recovering from mumps while poor Harold has unluckily just succumbed for Christmas.

The North Staffordshire Railway built the Churnet Valley line (1849) and the branch from Rocester to Ashbourne (1852). The junction had a single platform until 1885. J.W. Walker commented in 1911 that on local market days, compartments filled with passengers averaging 'three large baskets of eggs, butter and live fowls per head.' Ashbourne passenger service ended in 1954; regular passenger trains on the Churnet line in 1960.

Rocester has so changed that much shown in our old photographs has disappeared. The old bridge across the Churnet, the weir and former cotton workers' houses in Churnet Row remain. The corn mill is now converted to offices but the water wheel, seen here, has gone.

Fewer changes are apparent in High Street. The clock was over the now demolished shop of George Slaney, hairdresser and jeweller. The Red Lion remains and Buntings of Uttoxeter made sure you knew it was their pub. The 1888 Methodist chapel is now the Archaeological Centre where finds from Rocester's past are collected. The fenced area provides a community centre car park.

Looking the other way only The Red Lion survives. On the opposite corner was The Cross Keys, while whatever faults some old properties beyond in Mill Street may have had, at least they had character. Of some post-war rebuilding here, no comment – but big improvements are promised for the centre of Rocester in the near future. This picture is from the early 1920s.

The junction revealed this view down Ashbourne Road (The Cross Keys, extreme right). It is now extensively altered right down to The Queen's Arms. Only the cottages (left) remained at the time of writing, adapted as a supermarket with one pair boarded up. However, in 1906 you could at least stand around safely in the road.

The Queen's Arms (with wall rings to accommodate customers' horses) survives on the corner of Church Street, now opened out on the right and built up. Behind the cart a sign explains the tall pole: 'You may telephone from here'. This was the Post, Money Order and Telegraph Ofice where you could also collect letters on Sundays between 8.30 and 10.00am.

A look back (*c.* 1912) to the meeting point of the three principal streets to complete a picture of the centre of Edwardian Rocester. Slaney's shop faces (far right).

COTTON MILL, ROCESTER.

Rocester mill, under various owners, was the major local employer since being built by Sir Richard Arkwright in 1782. When Tutbury mill closed (1888) some families moved to Rocester and Aubrey Bailey recorded the 1894 winter when Tutbury folk skated up the Dove to visit friends. The mill finally closed in 1990 but has now been bought by JCB Excavators Ltd.

An Edwardian vista shows the extent of Croxden Abbey ruins and the pleasant countryside surrounding them. Bertram de Verdun of Alton founded Croxden in 1176 and building continued until the fourteenth century. It became noted for Staffordshire's finest wool before suppression in 1538. Most buildings were dismantled, 'old tymber and the roffe of the Churche' sold for £6. Later a public roadway was diverted through the remains. (English Heritage site).

On the fringes of our area the triassic sandstone which outcrops around Hollington has long provided quality building material, the quarries supplying stone for use locally and for major national projects – for example, the reconstruction of Coventry Cathedral. McCann's photograph shows stone cutting in progress around 1908 with massive blocks being lifted by quite primitive equipment – and not a safety helmet in sight!

The cross commemorates Sir Thomas Percival Heywood who gave Denstone its church, lychgate, vicarage and school; and was prominent in establishing Denstone College. Today a bus shelter, village hall and car park adjoin. There is now an open view of The Tavern (dated 1669). Here the Walker family provided the licensee over several generations. Behind this viewpoint the war memorial remembers fourteen local men and 237 College old boys.

Routes of packhorse trails and saltways sometimes survive as old names or in traces on the ground. These two hollows with outside mounds near Denstone (locally called Oliver's mounds) were probably formed on a packhorse way, the left-hand hollow being a diversion around wet or muddy ground. Mr W. Bernard Smith, Senior Science Master at Denstone College, used this McCann photograph in his school text book on Staffordshire (1915).

Denstone College was built on a site given by Sir Thomas Percival Heywood. The first stone was laid by Canon Lonsdale in 1868 and it opened as St Chad's College in 1873. This contemporary engraving was inserted in an unknown youngster's scrap book of that period. It

continues today as an Independent Co-Educational Day and Boarding School with a
Preparatory School at Smallwood Manor, Uttoxeter.

A Denstone College photograph with a poignant tale to tell. Rev R.M. Clark became Housemaster of Lowe House in 1897 and this scene records the end of his Housemastership in July 1914. Judging by the trophies on display his house put up some fine performances in his final year. Tragically, many of those in the photograph were soon to be victims of the First World War. The group is named as follows: Peel, Pattison, Dearmaley, Podmore, Keble, Pearce, Gregory, Embry, Bloomer, Lowndes and Seddon. Scarratt, Coggill, Evered, Keble, Dawson, Baness, Wood, Steel, Collis, Peacock, Podmore and Hardy. Dunnicliffe, Mitchell, Rev R.M. Clark, Musker and Taylor. Rose, Butcher, Johns, Punton and Stennett. Trophies include Senior football and cricket flags, and Junior football, Victor Ludorum, cross country and shooting cups and shields.

The Tuckshop, Denstone College

The postcard message is 'The tuckshop as it was' but it survived until 1960 and the display cabinet, right, is still used. Contents and advertising probably date this view to between the wars. Cadbury's products predominate with MacFarlane, Lang & Co's biscuit tins (Shortcake and Granada). There are sticky buns, left, with Camp Coffee and an intriguing range of tins and bottles but no crisps yet! Note lighting by paraffin lamp.

DOVELEYS, UTTOXETER. II M°CANN. Ph.

Doveleys, originally a small farm, was rebuilt by Thomas Percival Heywood in 1856 as his country house. He succeeded to the knighthood in 1856. His son, Sir Arthur Percival Heywood of Duffield Bank near Derby, well-known as a narrow-gauge railway engineer, made his first experiments at Doveleys which, after 1946, became an educational establishment. Formerly a Manchester family, there is Doveleys Road and Denstone Road in Eccles.

Raking hay (c. 1914) in front of the Quixhall entrance to Alton Towers, a free-standing arch between two lodges. A Victorian guidebook says: 'Quicksall [sic] Lodge ushers visitors into a magnificent approach to the house known as the Earl's Drive, three miles in length and leading along the Churnet valley.' Alton Towers grounds were then open in summer, admission 5p. The house was occupied until 1924. This is now the paved entrance to a private estate.

With the Weaver Hills and close proximity to Alton Towers and Dovedale this is a popular tourist area. This fine 1920s caravan and picnic scene was in a local collection. Although we cannot pin-point location or participants, the vehicle has the Staffordshire registration letter E. Unfortunately county records of early car owners previous to E6437 have not survived. Formal dress, substantial furniture and domestic service make this occasion almost like being at home.

A winter's day in Ellastone early this century photographed by H.P. Hansen (Ashbourne). The man delivering milk churns could safely proceed in the middle of the road. Just beyond him, right, is Ellastone Old Hall, later the Bromley Arms inn, reputedly envisaged by George Eliot as The Donnithorne Arms. The church lost a pinnacle in 1976 and the others were then removed.

These cottages remain in the centre of Ellastone but no longer house the local post office where one window was adapted to act as the letter box. Note the pump for water supply and the loft door open for ventilation on this sunny day.

In 1543 John Fleetwood converted Calwich Priory into a residence. A later Fleetwood, Sir Richard, built Wootton Lodge, one of the county's finest houses. Ellastone Church register records his marriage to a girl of <u>six</u>. In the early eighteenth century, Bernard Granville rebuilt Calwich where his guests included Rousseau and Handel. A fishing temple survives by the Dove but in 1846 William Burn rebuilt Calwich yet again for the Hon. Rev. A. Duncombe. This house, seen here, was largely demolished in 1928.

UTTOXETER and ASHBOURNE

Down	mn	Wk Days aft						Sun.				Miles	Up	mn	Week Days aft						Su
HOUR		A 8	A 9	12	S 3	E 5	S 5	7	8	aft 3	3	A 6 9		HOUR		7	9 11	1	4	S 7	9	aft 2 6 A
Uttoxeter ....dep.	23	56	.	50	12 10	43	0 36	.	.	0 35	.	—		Ashbourne ....dep.	25	2 36	.	40 25	.	20 15	.	30 0
Rocester..................	30	3	.	57	19 17	50	8 43	0	8 43 22				1½	Clifton, for Mayfield.....	28	5 39	.	43 28	.	24 18	.	34 3
Norbury and Ellaston....	37	10	.	4	26 24 57	16 50		6	15 50 28				4½	Norbury and Ellaston...	35	12 46	.	50 35	.	31 25	.	41 10
Clifton, for Mayfield.....	44	17	.	11	33 31 4	23 57		13	27 57 35				6½	Rocester 519.............	41	18 52	.	56 41	.	37 31	.	47 16
Ashbourne 523 .....arr.	49	23	.	16	38 36	9 28	2	18	34 2 40				11½	Uttoxeter 526, 528.arr.	50 28	1	.	5 50	.	45 40	.	25

A Through Trains to and from Buxton, page 523.   E Except Sats.   S Sats only

OTHER TRAINS between Uttoxeter & Rocester, p 519

Where the MINUTES under the Hours change to a LOWER figure and DARKER type it indicates the NEXT HOUR

The branch railway from Rocester to Ashbourne (1852) ran just over six miles up the Dove Valley, mostly single track and within Derbyshire. It closed for passengers in November 1954 and for goods in June 1964. The two intermediate stations were Norbury and Ellastone; and Clifton. The LMS timetable shows the 1938 service. On the Churnet line there was Denstone station 'for Croxden Abbey Ruins, Denstone College, and the Weaver Hills.'

A formal group by F.D. Palmby, junior, of Ellastone c. 1904. The gentlemen are all smokers – presumably Players Navy Cut if we examine the items on the bamboo table. The mongrel has been persuaded to sit still facing the camera and the photographer has solved the problem of what to do with hands by suggesting a flower, a book, and a walking stick.

A gentle scene on the winding road leading up the dale from Ellastone to the Weaver Hills and the hamlet of Stanton. This is remote and delightful country, the road passing Ouseley Wood and the fragment of an old cross. Apart from thicker woodland seventy years have left this scene virtually unchanged.

Three thousand years of history are recalled in this 1922 photograph inscribed 'A lovely day at Ramshorn and on the Weaver hills. Climbed up to the bronze age barrows.' Up here on a clear day much of the area covered in this book is spread out below with landmarks visible as far as Burton and beyond.

Haymakers at Mayfield around the turn of the century. The horse was still supreme in a region that later produced so many mechanical aids to farming. Within the century, like much in this book, what was then a view of a timeless and unchanging scene has become, for many people, a picture of days beyond living memory.

Mayfield is widespread and a place of contrasts. This group of three mills (once four) remains, along with terraces of houses built for mill workers between 1856 and 1872. Around the church (Church Mayfield) it is village rather than townscape. Middle Mayfield has its own little crescent of a lane and one looks for Tom Moore's cottage at Upper Mayfield.

This is Church Mayfield, 1903. It remains a rural backwater on a lane running parallel to the main road but with new housing opposite the church. This has a tower dating from 1515 but various periods are represented from late Norman onwards. In the nineteenth century the post office was officially using the name Maghfield (and for Mayfield's Sussex namesake).

Where Staffordshire and Derbyshire meet, Hanging Bridge and Gallowtree Hill are reminders of a boundary where wrong-doers were brought for execution. The Medieval pack horse bridge has twice been widened, firstly to cater for coaches and then again to cope with the demands of motor traffic. Milk churns by the signpost were awaiting collection from the Mayfield Dairy Association.

Looking into Derbyshire after crossing the bridge, the first building is The Royal Oak. The view (c. 1903) leaves no doubts about it being supplied by Salt's brewery of Burton. There is also the wheel symbol of the Cyclists Touring Club. Early enthusiasts were warned, 'care is necessary descending to Mayfield with a stiff climb if heading out to Leek.' Either way probably warranted dismounting for refreshment.

The length of the bridge at Mayfield was necessitated by the dividing of the Dove to provide a mill race and a weir. This view shows the water wheel at the corn mill of Frank Wright – 'corn, oatcake, sand, manure and coal merchant; grain warehouse and coal wharves.' Now only the ruined mill race and a few foundations and steps remain but there is a good view of an earlier arch incorporated under the reconstructed bridge.

An interesting group photograph from the Mayfield area and, like the haymakers, typical of its day and very much an image of times past. Here is the sort of domestic staff that might be found in a modest country house or possibly at some sort of institution – half a dozen women as indoor servants and two men as outdoor workers. Those in the front, nevertheless, are almost certainly a little superior in the domestic hierarchy of the day.

At the northern extremity of East Staffordshire, close to Dovedale, is Okeover Hall (not open to the public) the restored Medieval church close by. It has remained within the same family for over 800 years. In Plot's *History of Staffordshire* (1686) we see a moated mansion on the present site. Rebuilding began in 1745 and further extensive remodelling and restoration of Okeover was completed in 1953–60.

Six

A Diary of Memorable Occasions

Lady Noreen Bass, a daughter of the Earl of Huntingdon, had married Sir W.A.H. Bass of Byrkley Lodge in 1903. She laid the foundation stone for Yoxall's new parish hall in November 1904. By August 1905 the hall was completed by local contractor Mr Wright at a cost of £800 and was duly opened, debt-free, by Lady Burton.

This photograph shows that occasion with Lady Burton accompanied by Lord Burton, posing with local officials. On 7 April 1906 Lady Burton was again at Yoxall to open the District Co-operative Dairy premises, converted in ten weeks from a cottage, with 'the most up to date machinery from Messrs. Bamford of Uttoxeter.'

On Thursday 20 June 1907 Uttoxeter shops closed all day for the Trading Association outing arranged by Mr T.W. Orme. Members went by train to Rowsley, brakes and coaches taking over for visits to Chatsworth and Haddon. McCann took this souvenir picture during a stop at The Devonshire Arms, Beeley. Tea was served at The Rutland Arms, Bakewell, so both noble families were twice honoured!

A large crowd attended the foundation ceremonies for Leigh Methodist Church at Dodsleigh in September 1908. Thirty-eight large stones record local families such as the Ratcliffes and Leasons along with visitors from Ellastone, Birmingham, Stoke, Hanley, and Matlock. Forty-four other blocks are inscribed with single names. At the entrance, stones were laid on behalf of the Sunday School, Christian Endeavour, and by the minister, Rev W.H.M. Matthews.

In the twelfth century, Robert de Ferrers created the parks of Barton and Dunstall out of Needwood Forest. This cheerful scene records a May Festival at Dunstall Hall in 1908. May Day once heralded traditional celebrations in the countryside – a custom having its roots in the honouring of Flora, Roman goddess of fruits and flowers.

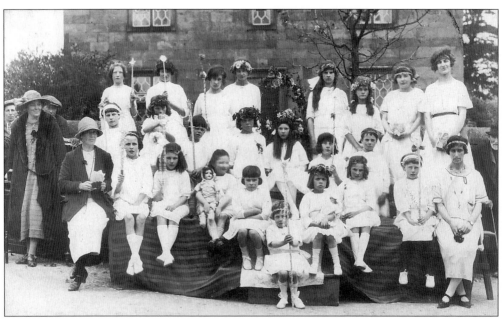

Stanton, high up on the Weaver Hills and one of the smallest parishes in East Staffordshire, provides another May Day celebration scene, photographed by Mossop of Mayfield. Although undated, costume styles suggest the early 1920s. The background was the School House and school buildings behind have become the Gilbert Sheldon Hall (see page 91). Behind again is Hillock Farm, Sheldon's birthplace.

A sunny July day in 1909 saw a large crowd in the courtyard of Tutbury Castle attending the local flower show. Burton Bijou Concert Party is providing the entertainment and a Mr Butterworth won first prize in the fancy dress parade as a 'flying machine'. Louis Bleriot had made the first cross-Channel flight just a few days before this event.

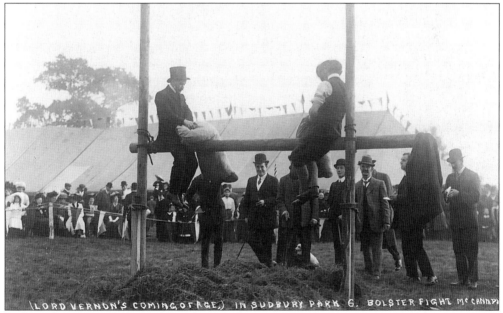

Sudbury lies in Derbyshire although its railway station was in East Staffordshire. Now by-passed, it attracts visitors for the Hall and the Museum of Childhood (National Trust). At Sudbury Hall on 1 October 1909 the 8th Baron succeeded to the Vernon estates. Following the customary feasting, presentations and speeches of those times, entertainments and events were staged in the park including this novel tournament of bolster fighting.

The 3rd Annual Festival of the Dove and Churnet Valleys Musical Competitions took place at Denstone College on Tuesday 12 April 1910. Here, Rocester Choral Society pose with the Philips Challenge Cup which they won with 71 points, Mayfield coming second with 69. A Rocester quartet also won the Challenge Banner with Denstone as runners-up.

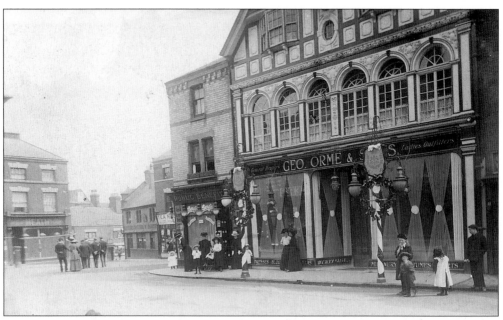

This Uttoxeter photograph describes Friday 20 May 1910 as 'the end of an era – the day King Edward VII was buried.' Orme's millinery department has empty windows draped in mourning with wreaths and black ribbons on the external gas lamps. Blinds are down at the Public Benefit Boot Company. Beyond, the Misses Heaths' ladies outfitting establishment on Bear Hill was soon to be demolished. Far right is The Spread Eagle which later became shops.

Crowds now line the streets to watch a procession to the Parish Church for the King's memorial service. Among contingents passing here are the military, post office staff (including telegram boys), scouts, Grammar School headmaster and top-hatted dignitaries. Blinds are down or shutters closed except at Hunter's with their elaborate window display and publicity for the new 'Hunta' margarine.

The good folk of Uttoxeter, arrayed in Sunday best, enjoying King George V's Coronation Day, 22 June 1911. To the left of Hankinson's shop is that of G.H. Smart who was 'printer, proprietor and publisher' of *The New Era*, Uttoxeter's oldest newspaper (1855) before its incorporation with *The Uttoxeter Advertiser* (1882) as from 4 May 1910.

The Pageant "Child Marriages"

In December 1922 various Uttoxeter groups staged a pageant entitled 'Children Through the Ages' to raise money for Waifs and Strays and the Church Hall and Insitute Fund. This scene was from 'Child Marriages' and portrayed the contrived wedding in 1478 of Richard, Duke of York to Lady Anne Mowbray when they were four and six years old respectively.

Whit Monday 1923

The Bishop of Lichfield is not, as may appear in this photograph, blessing Barclays Bank, which then used the end part of Abbots Bromley Church Room. This is the re-opening ceremony on Whit Monday 1923 when there was a procession to the war memorial for a service there. This attractive building (1619) has subsequently enjoyed further restoration.

While Uttoxeter's first carnival was in 1925, this is Rocester staging their 1922 event (1 July) on the cricket ground in front of Millholme, the house opposite the mill. Does anyone remember Noblett's Everton Toffee (see the basket, left)? Mr E. Birch as an Austrian Hussar accompanies Mrs Proctor as Queen Eleanor. S.A. Johnson of Rocester was the photographer.

The mill water tower can just be seen over the roof of Millholme in this picture of a carnival parade entry showing Heathcote's cart set out as a blacksmith's shop.

Uttoxeter's first carnival (1925) coincided with the opening of the Recreation Ground. Early events were presided over by a 'King and Queen' (Messrs. Shaw and Hodgkins). This is the 1927 'knighting' of Mr C. Needham on the race course after the procession paraded through the town. Photographer Alfred McCann is the Equerry (left) with Miss Edith Shaw as Court Jester and the Boden boys from Denstone as attendants.

Later a young lady was chosen to be Carnival Queen, riding in the procession with her escort. In 1929 Miss Grace Nash is in the coach loaned by Mrs Cavendish of Crakemarsh Hall, the house now a ruin alongside the road between Uttoxeter and Rocester.

'There was some snow for Christmas 1956. By chance we were in The White Hart that Christmas Eve. It was warm and cosy with seasonal decorations and jovial company. Then, first, the chef appeared carrying a boar's head; and soon after came a motley little group with simple additions to their everyday clothes, who enthusiastically embarked on the old traditional mummers' tale of St. George and the Dragon. They were, of course, the local guisers and when we finally went into the frosty, moonlit night, with the bells ringing, we felt that Uttoxeter had given us a memorable Christmas Eve.' The Guisers that night were leader Bert Crutchley (a race course groundsman) close relatives Edward, Tod and Sid Crutchley, and Fred Johnson. Happily this old custom still survives – and long may it continue.

The Dove in Winter by Alfred McCann, *c.* 1910.

Acknowledgements

Tony Brenan; Burton upon Trent Public Library; *Burton Daily Mail*; Cambridge University Press for permission to use the photograph of Olivers's Mound from *Staffordshire* by W. Bernard Smith (1915); Chris Copp, County Museum Service; Dudley Fowkes, Staffordshire County Archivist; Mrs Doris Hamlin (Castle Cary); Sheffield Library and Information Services; Edmund and Bernard Stonier; Michael Swales (Old Denstonian Club); *Uttoxeter Advertiser*.

We have included within the text names of known photographers whose pictures make it possible to compile a period anthology such as this.

We are also grateful to many people we have met who helped us with suggestions and information. We always welcome hearing from readers who can correct or add to our archive records.